PURSUED
by
Love Everlasting

FOCUS ON THE FAMILY

Compiled by William Jensen

HARVEST HOUSE PUBLISHERS
EUGENE, OREGON

Pursued by Love Everlasting

Copyright © 1999 by Focus on the Family®

Published by Harvest House Publishers

Eugene, Oregon 97402

Focus on the Family® is a registered trademark of Focus on the
Family, Colorado Springs, CO 80995. For more information,
please contact:

> Focus on the Family
> Colorado Springs, CO 80995
> 1-800-A-Family
> www.family.org

ISBN 0-7369-0043-8

Design and production by Koechel Peterson and Associates, Minneapolis, Minnesota

Focus on the Family® and Harvest House Publishers have made every effort to trace
the ownership of all quotes and poems. In the event of a question arising from the use
of any quote or poem, we regret any error made and will be pleased to make the
necessary correction in future editions of this book.

Scripture quotations are from the New American Standard Bible, © 1960, 1962, 1963,
1968, 1971, 1972, 1973, 1975, 1977 by The Lockman Foundation. Used by permission.

Printed in the United States of America.

99 00 01 02 03 04 05 06 07 08 / IP / 10 9 8 7 6 5 4 3 2 1

I have loved you with an

everlasting love;

EVERLASTING

Therefore I have drawn you

with lovingkindness...

Love

C O N T E N

T S

Sweet
INF

LU ENCES

I never had the experience of looking for God.

It was the other way round;

He was the hunter...and I was the deer.

He stalked me...took unerring aim, and fired.

C. S. Lewis
Christian Reflections

Our whole being by its very nature is one vast need;

incomplete, preparatory, empty yet cluttered,

crying out for Him who can untie things

that are now knotted together

and tie up things that are still dangling loose.

C.S. LEWIS
The Four Loves

You were bought with a price, and what has cost God

For the sake of each

A It is sooner or later found that the most perfect love cannot utterly satisfy the heart of man. All our human intercourse, blessed and helpful as it may be, must be necessarily fragmentary and partial. The solitude of life in its ultimate issue is because we were made for a higher companionship. It is just in the innermost sanctuary, shut to every other visitant, that God meets us. We are driven to God by the needs of the heart.

Hugh Black

U E N C E S

much cannot be cheap.

of us He laid down His life, no less than the universe.

DIETRICH BONHOEFFER

There have been implanted in man an instinct

and a need which make him discontented till

he find content in God…The human heart has

ever craved for a relationship, deeper and

more lasting than any possible among men, undisturbed by change,

unmenaced by death, unbroken by fear, unclouded by doubt.

Hugh Black

INFLU

Be embraced, ye millions!

This kiss to the whole world!

Brothers—above the canopy of stars

Surely a loving Father dwells.

Do you fall headlong, o millions?

Do you sense the Creator, World?

Seek Him above the canopy of stars!

Above the stars He must dwell.

FRIEDRICH SCHILLER

The greatest thing about any

civilization is the human person,

and the greatest thing about this

person is the possibility of his

encounter with the person of

Jesus Christ.

Charles Malik

Thou has made us for Thyself,

O God, and we are restless

until we find our rest in Thee.

SAINT AUGUSTINE

Christ Jesus came into the world to save sinners.

THE APOSTLE PAUL

An "impersonal God"—well and good. A subjective God of beauty, truth and goodness, inside our own heads—better still. A formless life-force surging through us, a vast power which we can tap—best of all. But God Himself, alive, pulling at the other end of the cord, perhaps approaching at an infinite speed, the hunter, king, husband— that is quite another matter.... There comes a moment when people who have been dabbling in religion ("Man's search for God!") suddenly draw back. Supposing we really found Him? We never meant it to come to that! Worse still, supposing He had found us?

C.S. LEWIS
Miracles

Across the chasm of eighteen hundred years Jesus Christ makes a demand which is beyond all others difficult to satisfy. He asks for that which a philosopher may often seek in vain at the hands of his friends, or a father of his children, or a bride of her spouse, or a man of his brother. He asks for the human heart; He will have it entirely to Himself; He demands it unconditionally, and forthwith His demand is granted. Its powers and faculties become an annexation to the empire of Christ. All who sincerely believe in Him experience that supernatural love towards Him. This phenomenon is unaccountable, it is altogether beyond the scope of man's creative powers. Time, the great destroyer, can neither exhaust its strength nor put a limit to its range.

NAPOLEON BONAPARTE

Thou must be emptied of that wherewith thou art full,

that thou mayest be filled with that whereof thou art empty.

ST. AUGUSTINE

The most important part of our task will be to tell everyone who will listen that Jesus is the only answer to the problems that are disturbing the hearts of men and nations. We shall have the right to speak because we can tell from experience that His light is more powerful than the deepest darkness...How wonderful that the reality of His presence is greater than the reality of the hell about us.

BETSIE TEN BOOM, TO HER SISTER, CORRIE, IN A NAZI PRISON CAMP
The Hiding Place

"O God,...Thou seest how much I need Thee to come close to me, to put Thy arm round me, to say to me, *my child*: for the worse my state, the greater my need of my Father who loves me. Come to me, and my day will dawn; my love will come back, and, oh! How I shall love Thee, my God! And know that my love is Thy love, my blessedness Thy being."

GEORGE MACDONALD

As the sensation of hunger presupposes food to satisfy it, so the sense of dependence on God presupposes His existence and character.

OCTAVIUS BROOKES FROTHINGHAM

Some years ago one of the world's renowned scholars of the classics, Dr. E.V. Rieu, completed a great translation of Homer into modern English for the Penguin Classics series. He was sixty years old, and he had been an agnostic all his life. The publisher soon approached him again and asked him to translate the Gospels. When Rieu's son heard this he said, "It will be interesting to see what Father will make of the four Gospels. It will be even more interesting to see what the four Gospels make of Father." He did not have to wonder very long. Within a year's time E.V. Rieu, the lifelong agnostic, responded to the Gospels he was translating and became a committed Christian.

R. KENT HUGHES

I believe in the forgiveness of sins.
THE APOSTLES CREED

All Things

BEC

Can you not remember, dearly beloved, that day of days,

that best and brightest of hours, when first you saw the Lord,

lost your burden, received the roll of promise, rejoiced in full salvation,

and went on your way in peace? My soul can never forget

that day . . . What delight filled my soul!—what mirth,

OMENEW

what ecstasy, what sound of music and dancing,

what soarings to Heaven, what heights and depths

of ineffable delight! Scarcely ever since then have

I known joys which surpassed the rapture of that first hour.

Charles Spurgeon

For He loved mankind. And therefore did He die, as the

bridegroom who hath gone forth to save his bride from the hands

of robbers...Then did I understand that this mighty love upholdeth

all things in the world...For if God would, He could take the soul,

by force—we should be strengthless motes in His hand. But He

loves us as the bridegroom loves his bride, who will not force

her...God will find you...Be still, and fly not from Him who hath

sought after you before you were conceived in your mother's womb.

Sigrid Undset

BECO

All Things

Once we've tasted being alive, we can't go back
to being dead. Aliveness in God is addictive.

NANCY GROOM

For me, Christianity was not a "leap into the dark" but rather a "leap into the light." I took the evidence that I could gather and put it on the scales. The scales tipped the way of Christ being the Son of God and resurrected from the dead. It was so overwhelmingly leaning to Christ that when I became a Christian, it was a "leap into the light" rather than a "leap into the darkness." If I would have exercised "blind faith," I would have rejected Christ and turned my back on all the evidence.

JOSH MCDOWELL
Evidence that Demands a Verdict

God pardons like a mother, who kisses the offense into everlasting forgiveness.
Henry Ward Beecher

Faith does not spring from the miracle but the miracle from faith.

FYODOR DOSTOEVSKY

In the Trinity Term of 1929 I gave in, and admitted that God was God, and knelt and prayed; perhaps, that night, the most dejected and reluctant convert in all England. I did not then see what is now the most shining and obvious thing; the Divine humility which will accept a convert even on such terms...Who can duly adore that Love which will open the high gates to a prodigal who is brought in kicking, struggling, resentful, and darting his eyes in every direction for a chance of escape?...The hardness of God is kinder than the softness of men, and His compulsion is our liberation.

C. S. Lewis
Surprised by Joy

After six years given to the impartial investigation of Christianity, as to its truth or falsity, I have come to the deliberate conclusion that Jesus Christ was the Messiah of the Jews, the Saviour of the world, and my personal Saviour.

LEW WALLACE

The thing that awakens the deepest well of gratitude

in a human being is that God has forgiven sin. Paul

never got away from this. When once you realize all

that it cost God to forgive you, you will be held as in

a vise, constrained by the love of God.

OSWALD CHAMBERS

We are today accepted in the

Beloved, absolved from sin,

acquitted at the bar of God. We

are even now pardoned; even

now are our sins put away; even

now we stand accepted in the

sight of God, as though we had

never been guilty.

CHARLES SPURGEON

Happy, therefore, is the man who has come to the end of

himself, his own ideas, his own efforts, his own determination

to be saved by his own obedience, and has acknowledged his

utter sinfulness, his hopeless inability, and has accepted

Christ as "the end of the law for righteousness."

W.H. GRIFFITH THOMAS

Let not it be imagined that the life
of a good Christian must be a life
of melancholy and gloominess; for
he only resigns some pleasures to
enjoy others infinitely better.

BLAISE PASCAL

In Him we have redemption through His blood, the forgiveness

of our trespasses, according to the riches of His grace.

THE APOSTLE PAUL

God creates out of nothing. Wonderful you say. Yes, to be sure, but He does what is still more wonderful: He makes saints out of sinners.

Soren Kierkegaard

MEN EW

God just came into my heart one afternoon while I was alone in the loft of our big barn.

GEORGE WASHINGTON CARVER

The Christian is not one who has gone all the way with Christ. None of us has. The Christian is one who has found the right road.

CHARLES ALLEN

Once upon a time, Mercy sat upon her snow-white throne, surrounded by the troops of love. A sinner was brought before her, whom Mercy designed to save. The herald blew the trumpet, and after three blasts thereof, with a loud voice, he said—"O heaven, and earth, and hell, I summon you this day to come before the throne of Mercy, to tell why this sinner should not be saved."

There stood the sinner, trembling with fear; he knew that there were multitudes of opponents who would press into the hall of Mercy, and with eyes full of wrath would say, "He must not, and he shall not escape; he must be lost!"

The trumpet was blown, and Mercy sat placidly on her throne, until there stepped in one with a fiery countenance; his head was covered with light; he spoke in a voice like thunder, and out of his eyes flashed lightning!

"Who art thou?" said Mercy.

He replied, "I am Law; the law of God."

"And what hast thou to say?"

"I have this to say," and he lifted up a stony tablet, written on both sides; "these ten commands this wretch has broken. My demand is blood..."

But Mercy smiled, and said, "Law, I will answer thee. This wretch deserves to die; justice demands that he should perish—I award thee thy claim." And oh! How the sinner trembles. "But there is One yonder who has come with me today, my King, my Lord; His name is Jesus; He will tell you how the debt can be paid, and the sinner can go free."

Then Jesus spake, and said, "O Mercy, I will do thy bidding. Take Me, Law; put Me in a garden; make Me sweat drops of blood; then nail Me to a tree; scourge My back before you; put Me to death; hang Me on the cross; let blood run from My hands and feet; let Me descend into the grave; let Me pay all the sinner oweth; I will die in his stead."

And the Law went out and scourged the Saviour, nailed Him to the cross, and coming back with his face all bright with satisfaction, stood again at the throne of Mercy, and Mercy said, "Law, what hast thou now to say?"

"Nothing" said he, "fair angel, nothing..."

"Stand thou here," said Mercy, "sit on my throne; I and thou together will now send forth another summons." The trumpet rang again.

"Come hither, all ye who have aught to say against this sinner, why he should not be acquitted"; and up comes another—one who often troubled the sinner, one who had a voice not so loud as that of the Law, but still piercing and thrilling—a voice whose whispers were like the cutting of a dagger.

"Who art thou?" says Mercy.

"I am Conscience; this sinner must be punished; he has done so much against the law of God that he must be punished; I demand it; and I will give him no rest till he is punished…"

"Nay," said Mercy, "hear me," and while he paused for a moment, she took a bunch of hyssop and sprinkled Conscience with the blood, saying, "Hear me, Conscience, 'The blood of Jesus Christ, God's Son, cleanseth us from all sin,' Now hast thou ought to say?"

"No," said Conscience, "nothing…"

The trumpet rang a third time, and growling from the innermost vaults, up there came a grim black fiend, with hate in his eyes, and hellish majesty on his brows. He is asked, "Hast thou anything against that sinner?"

"Yes," said he, "…that man was always my friend; he listened ever to my insinuations; he scoffed at the gospel; he scorned the Majesty of heaven; is he to be pardoned, whilst I repair to my hellish den, forever to bear the penalty of guilt?"

Said Mercy, "Avaunt, thou fiend; these things he did in the days of his unregeneracy; but this word 'nevertheless' blots them out. Go thou to thy hell; take this for another lash upon thyself—the sinner shall be pardoned, but thou—never, treacherous fiend!"

And then Mercy, smilingly turning to the sinner, said, "Sinner, the trumpet must be blown for the last time!" Again it was blown, and no one answered. Then stood the sinner up, and Mercy said, "Sinner, ask thyself the question—ask thou of heaven, of earth, of hell—whether any can condemn thee?"

And the sinner stood up, and with a bold loud voice said, "Who shall lay anything to the charge of God's elect?…God?"

And the answer came. "No; He justifieth."

"Christ?"

Sweetly it was whispered, "No; He died."

Then turning round, the sinner joyfully exclaimed, "Who shall separate me from the love of God, which is in Christ Jesus our Lord?"…

No longer did the trumpet ring, but angels rejoiced, and heaven was glad, for the sinner was saved.

CHARLES SPURGEON

Remember that to the new heart there is a joy even sweeter than that of being forgiven, even the joy of forgiving others. The joy of being forgiven is only that of a sinner and of earth: the joy of forgiving is Christ's own joy, the joy of heaven.

Andrew Murray

All Things

BECO

If any man is in Christ, he is things passed away; behold,

THE APOSTLE PAUL

And today, if my eye of faith be dim, and I can

scarce see the precious blood, so as to rejoice that

I am washed in it, yet God can see the blood, and

as long as the undimmed eye of Jehovah looks upon

the atoning sacrifice of the Lord Jesus, He cannot

smite one soul covered in the scarlet mantle.

CHARLES SPURGEON

a new creature; the old

new things have come.

Grace comes free of charge to
people who do not deserve it—
and I am one of those people.

PHILIP YANCEY
What's So Amazing About Grace?

With an
EVER

Jesus is more ready to pardon than you are to sin,

More willing to supply your wants

Than you are to confess them.

Never tolerate low thoughts of Him.

LASTING

LOVE

You may study, look, and meditate,

But Jesus is a greater Savior than you think Him to be

When your thoughts are at their highest.

Charles Spurgeon

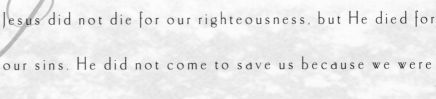

*I*esus did not die for our righteousness, but He died for our sins. He did not come to save us because we were worth saving, but because we were utterly worthless, ruined, and undone. He did not come to earth out of any reason that was in us, but solely and only because of reasons which He took from the depths of His own divine love. In due time He died for those whom He describes not as godly but as *ungodly*, applying to them as hopeless an adjective as He could have selected.

Charles Spurgeon

Let us but feel that He has His heart set upon us, that He is watching us from those heavens with tender interest, that He is following us day by day as a mother follows her babe in his first attempt to walk alone, that He has set His love upon us, and in spite of ourselves is working out for us His highest will and blessing, as far as we will let Him and then nothing can discourage us.

A. B. SIMPSON

Batter my heart, three personed God; for you

As yet but knock, breathe, shine, and seek to mend;

That I may rise and stand, o'erthrow me and bend

Your force to break, blow, burn and make me new.

I, like an usurped town, to another due,

Labour to admit you, but Oh, to no end;

Reason, your viceroy in me, me should defend,

But is captived and proves weak or untrue.

Yet dearly I love you and would be loved fain,

But am betrothed unto your enemy:

Divorce me, untie or break that knot again,

Take me to you, imprison me, for I

Except you enthrall me, never shall be free,

Nor ever chaste, except you ravish me.

JOHN DONNE

God suffers because He wills to love.

DENNIS NGIEN

God's own heart suffered on the cross.
Karl Barth

Yes, Jesus loves me, Yes, Jesus loves me,

Yes, Jesus loves me, The Bible tells me so.

ANNA BARTLETT WARNER

As the Father has loved Me,

I have also loved you.

JESUS

ING LOVE

The bride eyes not her garment,

But her dear Bridegroom's face;

I will not gaze at glory,

But on my King of Grace:

Not at the crown He giveth,

But on His pierced hand.

The Lamb is all the glory

In Emmanuel's land.

ANNE ROSS COUSIN

God's unfailing love for us is an objective fact affirmed over and over in the Scriptures. It is true whether we believe it or not. Our doubts do not destroy God's love, nor does our faith create it. It originates in the very nature of God, who is love, and it flows to us through our union with His beloved Son.

Jerry Bridges
Trusting God

Thou art coming to a King. Large petitions with thee bring For His grace and power are such None can ever ask too much.

JOHN DONNE

Let us not forget that the crucifixion of Christ was, and was intended to be to all the intelligences of the universe, the most significant exhibition of the love of God. "Herein is love."

J. GILCHRIST LAWSON

I stand amazed in the presence

Of Jesus the Nazarene,

And wonder how He could love me,

A sinner, condemned, unclean.

How marvelous! How wonderful!

And my song shall ever be.

How marvelous! How wonderful!

Is my Savior's love for me.

CHARLES H. GABRIEL

Do you think it was self-denial for

the Lord Jesus to come down from

heaven to rescue a world? Was it

self-denial? No, it was love—love

that swallows up everything, and

first of all self.

NIKOLAUS LUDVIG VON ZINZENDORF

One of the most convenient hieroglyphics of God is a circle; and a circle is endless;

whom God loves, He loves to the end; and not for their own end, to their death, but

to His end; and His end is that He might love them still. JOHN DONNE

In the face of humanity's refusal to receive God's love, He persisted and persisted and persisted. One representative after another of God was abused and slain...

Finally He sent His Son. Spurgeon said, "If you reject Him, He answers you with tears; if you wound Him, He bleeds out cleansing; if you kill Him, He dies to redeem; if you bury Him, He rises again to bring resurrection. Jesus is love made manifest."

R. Kent Hughes

What His justice demanded,
His love provided.
W. H. GRIFFITH THOMAS

Amazing love! How can it be

That thou, my God, should'st die for me?

Charles Wesley

Oh the deep, deep love of Jesus,
Love of every love the best!...
The deep, deep love of Jesus—
'Tis a heaven of heavens to me;
And it lifts me up to glory,
For it lifts me to Thee!
SAMUEL TREVOR FRANCIS

Here is love,

that God sent His son,

His Son that never offended,

His Son that was always His delight.

Herein is love, that He sent Him to save sinners;

to save them by bearing their sins,

by bearing their curse, by dying their death,

and by carrying their sorrows.

Here is love, in that while we were yet enemies,

Christ died for us;

Yes, here is love,

in that while we were without strength,

Christ died for the ungodly.

JOHN BUNYAN

God, dying for man, I am not afraid of that phrase;
I cannot do without it.

P. T. FORSYTH

Only a suffering God can help.

Suffering is not a sign of weakness,

but entails a decision to love.

DIETRICH BONHOEFFER

Great is

The God of Abraham, the God of Isaac,

the God of Jacob, the God of the Christians,

is a God of love and consolation. He is a God who

fills the soul and heart of those He possesses.

OUR GOD

He is a God who makes them aware inwardly of

their wretchedness while revealing His infinite mercy...

He is One who fills them with humility,

joy, confidence and love.

Blaise Pascal

Someone is there, I realized. Someone is watching life as it unfolds on this planet. More, Someone is there who loves me. It was a startling feeling of wild hope, a feeling so new and overwhelming that it seemed fully worth risking my life on.

Philip Yancey
Disappointment with God

IS

The power lies in the grace of God and not in our faith. Great messages can be sent along slender wires, and the peace-giving witness of the Holy Spirit can reach the heart by means of a threadlike faith which seems almost unable to sustain its own weight.

CHARLES SPURGEON

Be Thou exalted, O Lord, in Thy strength; we will sing and praise Thy power.

King David

The manger is Heaven, yes,

greater than Heaven. Heaven

is the handiwork of this child.

AGATHIAS SCHOLASTICUS

A mighty fortress is our God.

MARTIN LUTHER

Great

OUR GOD

In [the knowledge of God] is a subject so vast that all

our thoughts are lost in its immensity; so deep that our

pride is drowned in its infinity...

But while the subject humbles the mind, it also expands

it...Nothing will so enlarge the intellect, nothing so

magnify the whole soul of man, as a devout, earnest,

continuing investigation of the great subject of the Deity.

CHARLES SPURGEON

This Jesus of Nazareth, without money and arms, conquered more millions than

Alexander, Caesar, Mohammed, and Napoleon; without science and learning,

He shed more light on things human and divine than all

philosophers and scholars combined; without the

eloquence of schools, He spoke such words beyond

the reach of orator or poet; without writing a single line,

He set more pens in motion, and furnished themes for more sermons,

orations, discussions, learned volumes, works of art, and songs of praise than

the whole army of great men of ancient and modern times.

Philip Schaff

O Holy Spirit,

As the sun is full of light, the ocean full of water,

Heaven full of glory, so may my heart be full of Thee.

PURITAN PRAYER

Great

IS

Jesus, Thou Joy of loving hearts!

Thou Fount of life! Thou Light of men!

From the best bliss that earth imparts,

We turn unfilled to Thee again.

ST. BERNARD OF CLAIRVAUX

The very word "God" suggests care, kindness, goodness; and the idea of God, in His infinity, is infinite care, infinite kindness, infinite goodness. We give God the name of good: it is only by shortening it that it becomes God.

HENRY WARD BEECHER

Glory be to God for dappled things—

For skies of couple-colour as a brinded cow;

For rose-moles all in stipple upon trout that swim;

Fresh-firecoal chestnut-falls; finches' wings;

Landscape plotted and pieced—fold, fallow, and plough;

And all trades, their gear and tackle and trim.

All things counter, original, spare, strange;

Whatever is fickle, freckled (who knows how?)

With swift, slow; sweet, sour; adazzle, dim;

He fathers-forth whose beauty is past change:

Praise Him.

GERARD MANLEY HOPKINS

Superficial minds see a resemblance between Christ and the founders of empires, and the gods of other religions. That resemblance does not exist. There is between Christianity and whatever other religions the distance of infinity...Everything in Christ astonishes me. His spirit overawes me, and His will confounds me. Between Him and whoever else in the world, there is no possible term of comparison. He is truly a being by Himself...

Napoleon Bonaparte

It would take more than a Jesus to invent a Jesus.

PHILIP SCHAFF

Great IS OUR

Here is a man who was born in an obscure village, the child of a peasant woman. He grew up in another village. He worked in a carpenter shop until He was thirty, and then for three years He was an itinerant preacher. He never owned a home. He never wrote a book. He never held an office. He never had a family. He never went to college. He never put His foot inside a big city. He never traveled two hundred miles from the place where He was born. He never did one of the things that usually accompany greatness. He had no credentials but Himself....While still a young man, the tide of popular opinion turned against Him. His friends ran away. One of them denied Him. He was turned over to His enemies. He went through the mockery of a trial. He was nailed upon a cross between two thieves. While He was dying His executors gambled for the only piece of property He had on earth—His coat. When He was dead, He was taken down and laid in a borrowed grave through the pity of a friend. Nineteen long centuries have come and gone and today He is the centerpiece of the human race and the leader of the column of progress. I am far within the mark when I say that all the armies that ever marched, all the navies that ever were built, all the parliaments that ever sat and all the kings that ever reigned, put together, have not affected the life of man upon this earth as powerfully as has that one solitary life.

AUTHOR UNKNOWN

Truly, Jesus Christ, the Christ of the Gospels, the Christ of history, the crucified and risen Christ, the divine-human Christ, is the most real, the most certain, the most blessed of all facts. And this fact is an ever-present and growing power which pervades the Church and conquers the world, and is its own best evidence, as the sun shining in the heavens. This fact is the only solution of the terrible mystery of sin and death, the only inspiration to a holy life of love to God and man, the only guide to happiness and peace. Systems of human wisdom will come and go, kingdoms and empires will rise and fall, but for all time to come Christ will remain "the Way, the Truth, and the Life."

Philip Schaff

Faith implies the cessation of self-dependence and the commencement of dependence upon another. There is no value of merit in faith, for it derives its efficacy, not from the person trusting, but from the person trusted.

W.H. GRIFFITH THOMAS

I know men and I tell you that Jesus Christ is no mere man. Between Him and every other person in the world there is no possible term of comparison. Alexander, Caesar, Charlemagne, and I have founded empires. But on what did we rest the creations of our genius? Upon force. Jesus Christ founded His empire upon love; and at this hour millions of men would die for Him.

NAPOLEON BONAPARTE

I am sorry for the men who do not read the Bible every day. I wonder why they deprive themselves of the strength and of the pleasure. It is one of the most singular books in the world, for every time you open it, some old text that you have read a score of times suddenly beams with a new meaning. There is no other book that I know of, of which this is true; there is no other book that yields its meaning so personally, that seems to fit itself so intimately to the very spirit that is seeking its guidance.

WOODROW WILSON

How easy for me to live with You, O Lord!

How easy for me to believe in You!

…You grant me the serene certitude that You exist and that You will take care…

ALEKSANDR SOLZHENITSYN

A
GLORI

OUS FAITH

No one else holds or has held the place

in the heart of the world which Jesus holds.

Other gods have been as devoutly worshipped; no other

man has been so devoutly loved.

John Knox

I may, I suppose, regard myself as a relatively successful man. People occasionally stare at me in the streets. That's fame. I can fairly easily earn enough money to qualify for admission to the higher slopes of the Internal Revenue Service. That's success. Furnished with money and a little fame, even the elderly, if they care to, may partake of friendly diversions. That's pleasure. It might happen once in a while that something I said or wrote was sufficiently heeded for to persuade myself that it represented a serious impact on the time. That's fulfillment. Yet, I say to you, and I beg you to believe me, multiply these tiny triumphs by millions, add them all up together, and they are nothing, less than nothing. Indeed, a positive impediment measured against one drip of that living water Christ offers to the spiritually thirsty, irrespective of who or what they are.

Malcolm Muggeridge

Pray remember what I have recommended to you, which is, to think often on God, by day, by night, in your business, and even in your diversions. He is always near you and with you, leave Him not alone...Do not then forget Him, but think on Him often, adore Him continually, live and die with Him—this is the glorious employment of a Christian; in a word, this is our profession, if we do not know it we must learn it.

BROTHER LAWRENCE

FAITH

He is no fool who gives up that which he cannot keep to gain that which he cannot lose.

JIM ELLIOT

Faith is to believe what we do not see, and the reward of this faith is to see what we believe.

SAINT AUGUSTINE

Lift up your heart to Him...at your meals, and

when you are in company: the least little

remembrance will always be acceptable to Him.

You need not cry very loud, He is nearer to us

than we are aware of.

Brother Lawrence

GLORIOUS

If ever the Divine appeared on earth, it was in the person of Christ. The

human mind, no matter how far it may advance in every other department,

will never transcend the height and moral culture of Christianity as it

shines and glows in the Gospels. I esteem the Gospels to be thoroughly

genuine, for there shines forth from them the reflected splendour of a

sublimity, proceeding from the person of Jesus Christ...

JOHANN VON GOETHE

The Christian faith is faith in Christ. Its value or worth is not in the one believing but in the one believed—not in the one trusting, but in the one trusted.

JOSH MCDOWELL
Evidence that Demands a Verdict

F A I T H

Practical Christianity is the manifestation of a new life; a spiritual (as distinct from intellectual and moral) life; a supernatural (as distinct from natural) life; it is a life of holiness and peace; a life of union and communion with God the Father, the Son and the Spirit; it is eternal life, beginning with regeneration and culminating in the resurrection.

PHILIP SCHAFF

Faith is a living, daring confidence in God's grace. It is so sure and certain that a man could stake his life on it a thousand times.

MARTIN LUTHER

The words of Christ...are read more, quoted more, loved more, believed more, and translated more because they are the greatest words ever spoken. And where is their greatness? Their greatness lies in the pure, lucid spirituality in dealing clearly, definitively, and *authoritatively* with the greatest problems that throb in the human breast; namely, Who is God? Does He love me? Does He care for me? What should I do to please Him? How does He look at my sin? How can I be forgiven? Where will I go when I die? How must I treat others? No other man's words have the appeal of Jesus' words because no other man can answer these fundamental human questions as Jesus answered them. They are the kind of words and the kind of answers we would expect God to give, and we who believe in Jesus' deity have no problem as to why these words came from His mouth.

Bernard Ramm

I can only approve of those who seek God with groans.

BLAISE PASCAL

GLORIOUS

There are stages of grace, but not of justification. The feeblest believer is

accepted with God. The realization of his acceptance may differ but not

the reality. "A little faith will bring a soul into heaven,

but strong faith will bring heaven into the soul."

W. H. GRIFFITH THOMAS

Man's ultimate destiny depends not

on whether he can learn new lessons

or make new discoveries and conquests,

but on his acceptance of the lesson

taught him close upon two thousand

years ago.

INSCRIPTION AT THE EASTERN ENTRANCE

OF ROCKEFELLER CENTER, NEW YORK CITY

I believe in Christianity as

I believe that the sun has

risen, not only because I see

it, but because by it I see

everything else.

C.S. LEWIS
The Weight of Glory

FAITH

He told His disciples that after His departure they should do greater works than He had done, and the centuries of Christianity have borne out the truth of this statement. Works greater in kind have been done, are being done.

Jesus Christ is doing more wonderful things today than ever He did when on earth, redeeming souls, changing lives, transforming characters, exalting ideals, inspiring philanthropies, and making them for best, truest, and highest in human life and progress.

We are therefore justified in calling attention to the influence of Christ through the ages as one of the greatest, most direct, and most self-evident proofs that Christianity is Christ...

W. H. Griffith Thomas

GLORIOUS

Give me the wings of faith to rise

Within the veil, and see

The saints above, how great their joys,

How bright their glories be.

ISAAC WATTS

The Bible is a book of faith, and a book of doctrine,

and a book of morals, and a book of religion,

of especial revelation from God.

DANIEL WEBSTER

FAITH

Faith is a living, bold trust in God's grace.

MARTIN LUTHER

Faith affirms what the senses do not affirm,
but not the contrary of what they perceive.
It is above, and not contrary to.

BLAISE PASCAL

If God announces the gift of righteousness apart from works, why do you keep mourning over your bad works, your failures?...On seeing your failures, you should say, I am nothing but a failure; but God is dealing with me on another principle altogether than my works, good or bad—a principle not involving my works, but based on the work of Christ for me.

William Newell

A man can no more take in a supply of grace for the future than he can eat enough for the next six months, or take sufficient air into his lungs at one time to sustain life for a week. We must draw upon God's boundless grace from day to day as we need it.

D.L. MOODY

I believe in one God

the Father Almighty,

maker of heaven and earth,

and of all things visible and invisible:

And in one Lord Jesus Christ, the only-begotten Son of God,

begotten, not made,

being of one substance with the Father,

by whom all things were made;

Who for us men and for our salvation came down from heaven,

and was incarnate by the Holy Spirit of the Virgin Mary,

and was made man,

and crucified also for us under Pontius Pilate;

He suffered and was buried, and the third day He rose again

according to the Scriptures,

and ascended into heaven, and sitteth on the right hand of the Father;

And He shall come again with glory

to judge the quick and the dead;

Whose kingdom shall have no end.

And I believe in the Holy Spirit, the Lord and giver of life,

who proceedeth from the Father and the Son,

who with the Father and the Son together is worshipped and glorified;

who spoke by the prophets.

And I believe in one universal and apostolic church;

I acknowledge one baptism for the remission of sins,

and I look for the resurrection of the dead,

and the life of the world to come.

Amen.

THE NICENE CREED

The FELL

The people of God are tough. For long centuries

those who belong to the world have waged war against

the way of faith, and they have yet to win…

OWSHIP OF

THE SAINTS

The way of faith is not a fad that is taken up in

one century only to be discarded in the next. It lasts.

It is a way that works. It has been tested thoroughly.

Eugene Peterson
*A Long Obedience in
the Same Direction*

Christianity has thus passed through many stages of its earthly life, and yet has hardly reached the period of full manhood in Christ Jesus. During this long succession of centuries it has outlived the destruction of Jerusalem, the dissolution of the Roman empire, fierce persecutions from without, and heretical corruptions from within, the barbarian invasion, the confusion of the Dark Ages, the papal tyranny, the shock of infidelity, the ravages of revolution, the attacks of enemies and the errors of friends, the rise and fall of proud kingdoms, empires, and republics, philosophical systems, and social organizations without number.

And, behold, it still lives, and lives in greater strength and wider extent than ever; controlling the progress of civilization and the destinies of the world; marching over the ruins of human wisdom and folly, ever forward and onward; spreading silently its heavenly blessings from generation to generation, and from country to country, to the ends of the earth. It can never die; it will never see the decrepitude of old age; but, like its divine founder, it will live in the unfading freshness of self-renewing youth and the unbroken vigor of manhood to the end of time, and will outlive time itself...

PHILIP SCHAFF

For where two or three have gathered together

in My name, there I am in their midst.

Jesus

The church of God is an anvil that has worn out many hammers.

H.L. HASTINGS

The final grounds of holy fellowship are in

God. Persons in the fellowship are related to

one another through Him, as all mountains go

down into the same earth. They get at one

another through Him.

THOMAS KELLY

Here springs, in its original freshness and purity, the living water of the new creation. Christianity comes down from heaven as a supernatural fact, yet long predicted and prepared for, and adapted to the deepest wants of human nature. Signs and wonders and extraordinary demonstrations of the Spirit, for the conversion of unbelieving Jews and heathens, attend its entrance into the world of sin. It takes up its permanent abode with our fallen race, to transform it gradually, without war or bloodshed, by a quiet, leaven-like process, into a kingdom of truth and righteousness.

Philip Schaff

FELLOWSHIP

Blest be the tie that binds Our hearts in Christian love.

JOHN FAWCETT

If we walk in the light as He Himself is in the light,

we have fellowship with one another, and the

blood of Jesus His Son cleanses us from all sin.

JOHN, *the disciple whom Jesus loved*

OF THE SAINT

The Christian church is not a congregation of righteous

people. It is a society of those who know they are not good.

DWIGHT E. STEVENSON

It is ingrained in us that we have to do exceptional things for God, but we do not. We have to be exceptional in the ordinary things of life, and holy on the ordinary streets, among ordinary people, and this is not learned in five minutes.

Oswald Chambers

FELLOWSHIP

Jesus let us in on an astonishing secret. God has chosen to change the world through the lowly, the unassuming, and the imperceptible...That has always been God's strategy, changing the world through the conspiracy of the insignificant.

TOM SINE *Mustard Seed Conspiracy*

The Church's one foundation

Is Jesus Christ her Lord;

She is His new creation

By water and the word:

From Heaven He came and sought her

To be His holy bride;

With His own blood He bought her,

And for her life He died.

Samuel J. Stone

Is any pleasure on earth as great as a circle of Christian friends by a fire?

C.S. LEWIS
Letters of C.S. Lewis

The chief trouble with the church is that you and I are in it.

CHARLES H. HEIMSATH

Burned but not consumed.

MOTTO OF THE CHURCH OF SCOTLAND

See how these Christians love one another.

TERTULLIAN

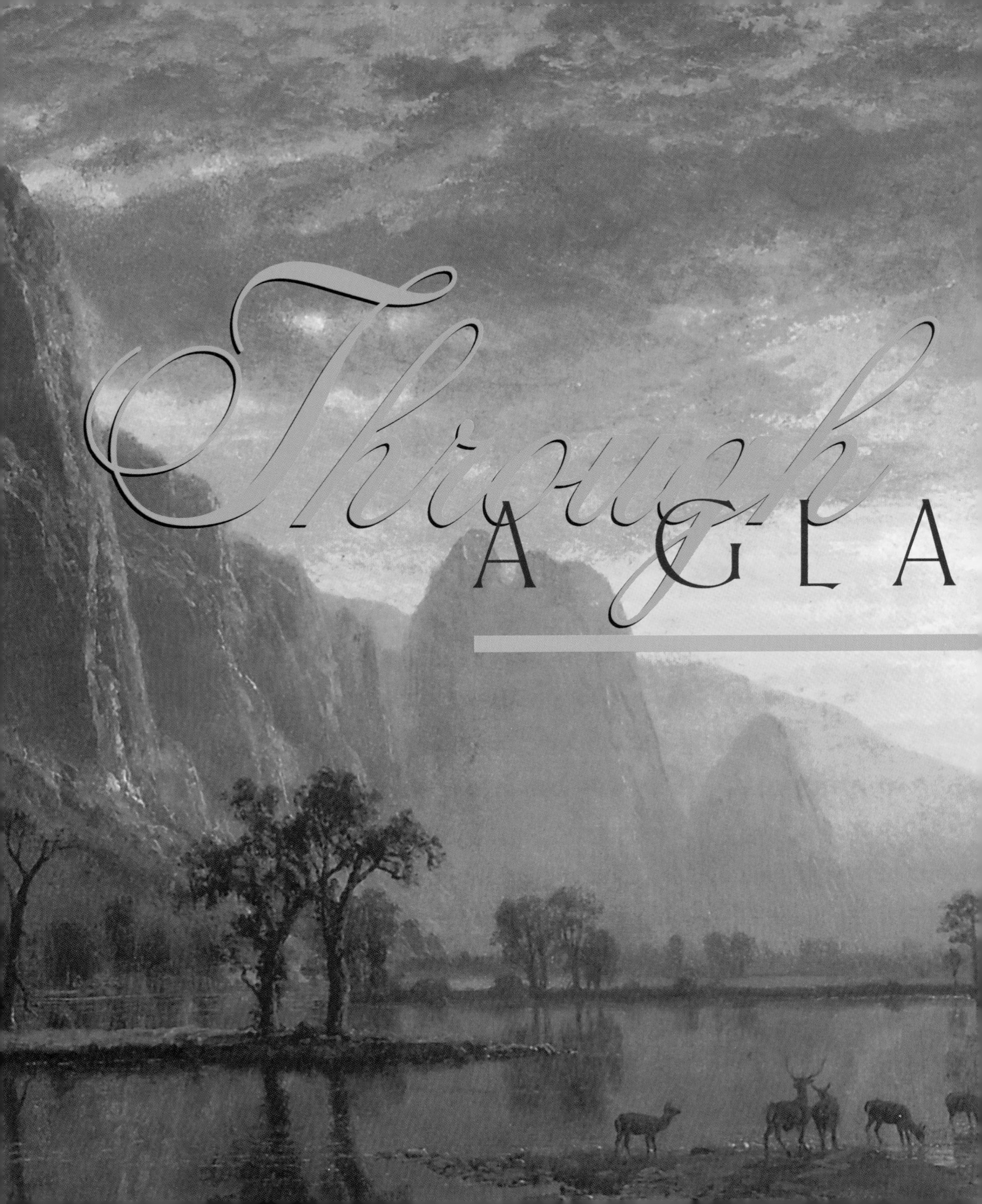
Through
A GLA

SS DARKLY

When we feel as if God is nowhere,

He is watching over us with an eternal consciousness,

above and beyond our every hope and fear.

George MacDonald

Let us therefore grant to the skeptics what they have so often proclaimed, that truth lies within our grasp, and yet it is not our prey. It does not dwell on earth, but has its home in heaven. It lies in the bosom of God, and so it can only be known insofar as it pleases Him to reveal it.

Blaise Pascal

There are moments in the life of all believers when God and His ways become unintelligible to them. They get lost in profound meditation, and nothing is left them but a desponding sigh. But we know from Paul the apostle that the Holy Spirit intercedes for believers with God, when they cannot utter their sighs.

AUGUSTUS F. THOLUCK

God discovers Himself to "babes" and hides Himself in thick darkness from the wise and prudent. We must simplify our approach to Him. We must strip down to essentials and they will be found to be blessedly few.

A. W. TOZER

God is God. If He is God, He is worthy of my worship, my trust, my obedience.

I am only a child, He is my Father. He will not explain everything, but I may find rest in His glorious will. His will is infinitely, immeasurable, ineffably beyond my largest notions of what He is up to, but I will find rest nowhere else.

ELISABETH ELLIOT
Through Gates of Splendor

The nature of Christ's existence is mysterious, I admit; but this mystery meets the wants of man—reject it and the world is an inexplicable riddle; believe it, and the history of our race is satisfactorily explained.

NAPOLEON BONAPARTE

What can be seen on earth indicates neither the total absence of God nor His manifest presence, but rather the presence of a hidden God.

BLAISE PASCAL

DARKLY

Wonder is the basis of Worship.

THOMAS CARLYLE

My mind had been so battered and was now so fatigued that I hardly knew how to think. Yet, as in that dark cell my vision cleared, I could not explain it nor did I need to do so. I knew that I believed my Saviour risen from the dead. I knew He was the Son of God. I knew He had shed His blood for me. I had been shaken, torn and wounded, but I was conscious still that round about me were His everlasting arms. I knew within my  heart the witness of His Spirit, triumphant still, standing yet inviolable to all the foe's assault.

I knew that underneath my feet, impregnable, unshaken and strong as ever, was the Rock of Ages, Jesus Christ my Lord.

And there as I sat, from the very wellsprings of my soul surged up the words that God is pleased to honour above all human utterance, "I believe."

Geoffrey T. Bull
missionary prisoner in Communist China

A GLASS

The Christian is a man who can be certain about the ultimate even when he is most uncertain about the immediate.

D. MARTYN LLOYD-JONES

I went to the theater with the author of a successful play. He insisted on explaining everything. He told me what to watch, the details of directions, the errors of the property man, the foibles of the star. He anticipated all my surprises and ruined the evening. Never again! And mark you, the greatest author of all made no such mistake.

CHRISTOPHER MORLEY

God has frequently to knock the bottom board out of your experience if you are a saint in order to get you into contact with Himself.

God wants you to understand this is a life of *faith*, not a life of sentimental enjoyment of His blessings....

"Though He slay me yet will I trust Him"—this is the most sublime utterance of faith in the whole of the Bible.

OSWALD CHAMBERS

For as sight is only seeing, so faith is only believing. And as the only necessary thing about sight is that you see the thing as it is, so the only necessary thing about faith is that you believe the thing as it is. The virtue does not lie in your believing, but in the thing you believe.

Hannah Whitall Smith

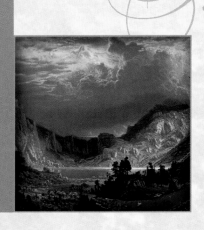

But this is not the way God has chosen to appear in the humility of His coming. Because, since so many have become unworthy of His mercy, He wished to deprive them of the good that they did not desire. It was therefore not right that He should appear before them in a manner that was obviously divine and absolutely bound to convince all mankind. Neither was it right that His coming should be in such hiddenness that He could not be recognized even by those who sincerely looked for Him. But He wished to make Himself perfectly recognizable to such. Instead, wishing to appear openly to those who seek Him with all their heart, and yet hidden from those who shun Him with all their heart, God has given signs of Himself, which are visible to those who seek Him, and not by those who do not seek Him.

Blaise Pascal

It is an exercise in sanity to trust Him. It is growing sanity to commit all of your life to Him. In the light of His claims and the full revelation of Scripture, any other life is crazy…The supremely sane life is one that is totally committed to Him.

R. KENT HUGHES

In our sad condition our only consolation

is the expectancy of another life.

Here below all is incomprehensible.

MARTIN LUTHER

Faith is like a radar which sees through the fog—the
reality of things at a distance that the human eye cannot see.

CORRIE TEN BOOM

For now we see in a mirror dimly,

but then face to face; now I know in part,

but then I shall know fully just as I also

have been fully known.

The Apostle Paul

DARKLY

I Shall
S   E

What reason have atheists for saying that we cannot rise

again? Which is more difficult—to be born, or to rise

again? That what has never been, should be,

E GOD

or that what has been, should be again? Is it more difficult

to come into being than to return to it again?

Blaise Pascal

This present life is momentary, but the state of

death is eternal. How terribly important it is,

then, to live in the light of the eternal, since it

ultimately affects all that we do or think! Since

nothing is more obvious than this observation,

how absurd it is to behave differently.

Blaise Pascal

I would rather die for
Christ than rule the whole
earth. Leave me to the
beasts that I may by them
be a partaker of God.

IGNATIUS, *who was thrown to the beasts*
in the coliseum in Rome

I have sent for you that you may see how a Christian can die.

JOSEPH ADDISON, *on his death bed, to his stepson*

Eighty and six years have I served Him, and He hath done me no wrong. How can I speak evil of my King who saved me?

POLYCARP, WHEN ASKED TO RECANT AND

LIVE.   HE WAS BURNED AT THE STAKE.

Death be not proud,

though some have called thee

Mighty and dreadful, for, thou art not so,

For, those, whom thou think'st,

thou dost overthrow,

Die not, poor death, nor yet canst thou kill me...

One short sleep past, we wake eternally,

And death shall no more; death, thou shalt die.

JOHN DONNE

Living is death; dying is life,

we are not what we appear

to be. On this side of the

grave we are exiles, on that

side citizens; on this side

orphans, on that side

children.

HENRY WARD BEECHER

We picture death as coming to destroy; let us rather picture Christ as coming to save. We think of death as ending; let us rather

think of life as beginning, and that more abundantly. We think of losing; let us think of gaining. We think of parting, let us think of meeting. We think of going away; let us think of arriving. And as the voice of death whispers, "You must go from earth," let us hear the voice of Christ saying, "You are but coming to Me!"

Norman Macleod Leaves of Gold

As organs in the Body of Christ, as stones and pillars in the temple, we are assured of our eternal self-identity and shall live to remember the galaxies as an old tale.

C. S. LEWIS *The Weight of Glory*

Let people think what they like, but the only good in life lies in the hope of another life. We are only happy in the measure to which we anticipate it, for there will be no misfortunes to those who are completely assured of eternal life.   BLAISE PASCAL

Abide with me: fast falls the eventide;

The darkness deepens; Lord, with me abide:

When other helpers fail, and comforts flee,

Help of the helpless, O abide with me!

Swift to its close ebbs life's little day;

Earth's joys grow dim, its glories pass away;

Change and decay in all around I see:

O Thou who changest not, abide with me!

I need Thy presence every passing hour:

What but Thy grace can foil the tempter's power?

Who like Thyself my guide and stay can be?

Through cloud and sunshine, O abide with me!

Hold Thou Thy word before my closing eyes;

Shine through the gloom, and point me to the skies:

Heaven's morning breaks and earth's vain shadows flee—

In life, in death, O Lord, abide with me!

H. F. LYTH

Here lies the body of John Smith, who for forty years cobbled shoes in this village to the glory of God.

JOHN SMITH'S EPITAPH

Father, I desire that they also, whom Thou hast given Me, be with Me where I am, in order that they may behold My glory, which Thou hast given Me; for Thou didst love Me before the foundation of the world.

JESUS

Be of good comfort, Master Ridley, and play the man. We shall this day light such a candle, by God's grace, in England, as I trust shall never be put out.

HUGH LATIMER TO DOCTOR RIDLEY

at their martyrdom in Oxford. They were burned at the stake.

Seems it strange that thou shouldst live forever? Is it less strange that thou shouldst live at all? This is a miracle; and that no more.

EDWARD YOUNG

To live is Christ, and to die is gain.

THE APOSTLE PAUL

Be faithful until death, and I will give you the crown of life.

JESUS

I know that my Redeemer lives.

JOB

Death borders

upon our birth, and

our cradle stands

in the grave.

BISHOP HALL

Well, the delightful day will come

When my dear Lord will bring me home,

And I shall see His face;

Then with my Saviour, Brother, Friend,

A blest eternity I'll spend,

Triumphant in His grace,

Triumphant in His grace.

Samuel Medley

When shall it ever happen,
When comes the welcome day
In which I shall behold Him
In all His majesty?
Thou day, when wilt thou be,
In which we greet the Savior,
In which we kiss the Savior?
Come, make thyself appear!
POET UNKNOWN

Who shall separate us from the love of Christ? Shall tribulation, or distress, or persecution, or famine, or nakedness, or peril, or sword? Just as it is written, "For Thy sake we are being put to death all day long; we were considered as sheep to be slaughtered."

But in all these things we overwhelmingly conquer through Him who loved us. For I am convinced that neither death, nor life, nor

angels, nor principalities, nor things present, nor things to come, nor powers, nor height, nor depth, nor any other created thing, shall be able to separate us from the love of God, which is in Christ Jesus our Lord.

The Apostle Paul